AF619592

HOW TO TAME A WILD TEMPEST

Helle Gade

BUTTERDRAGONS
PUBLISHING

Title: How To Tame A Wild Tempest

Author: Helle Gade

Published by Butterdragons® Publishing
https://butterdragons.com

ISBN: 9789493229488 (ebook)
ISBN: 9789493229495 (hardback)
ISBN: 9789493229501 (audio book)

Cover Design by: Dazed Designs

Audio book narrated by Martha Webb

To my mom, dad, and pap

for always supporting me.

For Helle, with love

Sweet girl, you have a heart of gold. I see your naked feet on coarse sand, dancing along the frothy crowns of waves. There are a million questions in your head, a million songs on your tongue. Your words ride on the wind, changing its tune to bouts of heartache and beauty. Where does this longing start? Where does it end? Your soul could encompass the world. Wants to travel everywhere. So stuck. So delicate.

Yet you stride on without fear, ignoring the fact that you could burst at any minute. Burst like the bubbles 'neath your toes.

Sweet girl, why are your words so sad? They kindle the embers of melancholy in my chest. And I want nothing more than to join you on the beach and hear your magic songs. You, siren of words.

Our hands would entwine like washed-up seaweed. Fingers sticky with salt and sand. I would walk with you. Forever.

Sweet girl, never forget you are loved. This world holds more beauty because you are in it.

by BDP Authors

Silent Dreams

Chaos

Frozen

Frozen in time
Watching the world churn and boil
Technology streaking by
In light speed
Constantly changing

Standing frozen
Unable to follow
Unable to move with the world
Left to the merciless pain
The numb living

Lost Days

I no longer remember
The days of ease
Of not having to fight
An invisible force

Challenges assail me
Force me to act
To change my way of thinking

How do I find joy in a sea of hurt?
Where is my laughter?
Where is my peace?

Order

Order and control
How I desire it
My world is chaotic
Not a thing in its place
Up and down reversed
Ill-fitting and broken

Question

Crumpling to the ground
Hugging myself
Taking rapid breaths
Trying to diminish the pain
What is my lesson?
Why am I here?
Seeking guidance
Seeking the Gods

Knowledge

I wonder what it is
That I'm supposed to learn
In this life
Where is my place?
What is my role?
This puzzle confuses me
I'm adrift in the wind
Not knowing
A mere drop
In the ocean of knowledge
Beyond my reach
And yet so close

Watching

The days passing me by
Life blooming and decaying
In front of me

I stand silently
Watching the world turn
Watching the seasons come and go

Out of time
Out of reality
Out of touch

I stand out
I make people laugh and cry
I give comfort
Yet none of it matters

I'm cold
Walls build around my mind
A true fortress of old
Defended by a slumbering fire dragon

Breach my defences
And you will burn

Therefore, I watch
Living in a separate world
Parallel to yours
Biding my time
Until the end

Out of time
Out of reach
Out of touch

Victory

I bear my pain with grace
Your scorn shall not bring me down
I am a warrior
A champion in my own right
I will fight to the end
My strength infinite
My compassion flowing

Nordic

Mother Moon

The icy wind biting my skin
The night closing in
The moon slowly rising on the horizon
The light of the Goddess bathing us in Her grace

Thunder and Mischief

As the thunderstorm approaches
Electricity fills the air
The scent of ozone is strong
Lightning flashes in the distance
Low rumblings of thunder sound overhead
They are getting closer
The wagon wheels creak
The goat hooves shooting sparks
As they chase through the sky
On the eternal hunt
I stretch my neck
Hoping for a glimpse of them
A secret wish
A childhood dream

Freya

Long flowing honey blond hair
Cornflower blue eyes
Promising wicked nights
Of carnal delights

Warrior

I watch them live
Occasionally, I join them
Fooling them expertly
They think me one of them
But oh, how wrong they are

I am the watcher
I catalogue their strengths and weaknesses
Biding my time until Ragnarok
The final fight for the world
The time of the Gods

I will put on my helmet
I will sharpen my weapons
I will ready myself for the kill
I will be victorious
I am the warrior
The bringer of death

They will not escape my icy wrath
Their blood will pool at my feet
And I will revel in their pain

The end is coming
Feel the fear creep up your spine
As I approach in all my glory

Your life is mine
Your blood my nourishment

The end is near
Say goodbye to your loved ones
For this is your last chance
I will watch as you do
There will be no mercy

Darkness

Haunted

Always there
Like burning flames
Waves crashing
A stabbing knife
Always there
In the back of my mind
Churning and burning
All consuming

Control

Your fingers gently trace
A path up my spine
Leaving burning pain in their wake
Stealing my breath
Leaving me too weak to scream
I writhe under your unrelenting attention
Hoping for mercy
Where none is to be found
Shedding my humanity
Leaving only an empty husk

Time

Time flies
As the bird cries
In the silent night
Soon to be forgotten
In the vast chasm
That is life

Torment

Claws ripping into my soft belly
Tearing the tender flesh
Digging deep into my abused body
I have no breath to scream
I'm immobilized by agony
Trapped
With nowhere to escape
The pain
Crashing over me in waves
Threatens to crush my frail mind
Insanity is moments away

Manic

Crying one moment
Laughing the next
The heart beats
To the executioner's drum
A tale of madness
And of decay

Stardust

His embrace
Chilling me to the bone
His eyes
Windows into the abyss
His kiss
The taste of graveyard dirt
His voice
Cutting my soul
His thoughts
The darkest arctic night

Release me, I scream
Forgive me, I beg
Finish me, I hope
Bleed me, I feel
Destroy me, I pray

His embrace
Now crushing
His eyes
Now soul shattering

His kiss

Now choking me

His voice

Now bleeding me

His thoughts

Now ending me

Disconnected

Floating

Freezing

Unbound

Dissolved

Whole no more

Mixing with the fallout

Of the supernova

Spreading through the universe

Once more perfect

Once more stardust

Joy

Dancing

The freedom of movement
The flow of kinetic energy
Music caressing the senses
As we fly above the polished floor
The gentle sweep of feathers
A hand guiding me
At the small of my back
The joy of being led
In mirrored movements
Of a kindred spirit

Solitude

In the dark night
Snowflakes falling slowly
In absolute silence

Blissful peace
The joy of solitude
Holding my book
Sipping my tea
Chocolate on my tongue

My heart is filled with contentment
Stroking silky fur beside me
Looking into dark brown eyes
That shine with devotion
Pure unconditional love

Immersing myself
In a foreign world
Living a life in hours
Laughing, crying, loving
In the dark of night
The joy of solitude

Silent Night

In the silent night
I ponder the flight
That is my life

A whispered word
A gentle touch
A thought of love

Stars bright
Fill me with light
In the silent night

Passion

Skin like burning gold
Soft as silk
Sweet as honey
Intoxicating and addictive

Bodies sliding together
Sensitive to every touch

Fingers caressing
Tongues dancing
Passion building
Making the skin flush
Trembling limbs
Moans erupting
Sweet pain
Ripping through our bodies
Connecting our souls
Bringing us a glimpse of the divine

Love

Fierce love
Reaches across worlds
To collide in fiery sparks
Leaving ripples in the Universe
Bringing hope to us all

Dreams

I dream in the night
I dream in the day
I dream with my eyes open
As well as closed
I dream of the stars
Of twirling galaxies
Of things out of my reach
And within my grasp
Of long forgotten times
And times yet to come
Of love and hope
A future so bright

Equestrian Bliss

Stroking the soft muzzle
Gripping the reins
Putting my foot in the stirrups
Getting into the saddle
The feeling of coming home

Calm settles over me
Energy shared with the soul beneath me
Instinctive communication

A tiny kick with my heel
Sets the creature in motion
I feel as an extension of it
Our movements flowing easily together
Exhilaration coursing through my veins

The horse feels my excitement
It starts to dance
Eager to run
To release the pent-up energy
To share the joy of freedom

Mother

She is a tiny woman
With a heart of gold
The strength of a goddess
And the soul of an angel

Her compassion divine
Her comfort healing
Her words soothing
Her love my world

I would be nothing without her
I am everything because of her
She is my guiding star
The light of my life

Far

Han er mild og blid
Med en humor sort som kul

Altid der, når behovet opstår
Aldrig et ondt ord at give

Han er min støtte
Han er min opmuntring
Han er min styrke
Han er min verden

Uden ham og hans sorte hest
Ville min sjæl være tom
Han er mit hjerte
Han er min far

Danmark

Mit hjem er under den rød og hvide fane
Langs det brusende hav
Under den grønne bøg
Blandt de stolte vikinger
Snor Gudenåen sig om mit hjerte
I den Østjyske muld

Nocturnal Embers

Winner of the Best Poetry Collection

eFestival of Words

Nocturnal Embers

Smouldering embers
In my mind
Burning away

Tiny flames
Kissing my fears
Surrounding my thoughts

The heat
Etching holes
Through memories

Devouring
What is left of me
A nocturnal creature

Burn
Burn
Burn

Writing

As the pen flies across the paper
My imagination soars to new heights
Dreams become written reality
Touching the souls of many
I bring unknown worlds into your life
Feelings and faces you'll never forget
I am but a drop in the world's imaginary ocean
But my voice carries power
The power to change myself
And perhaps the thoughts of others
The written word is my blessing
And my saviour

Memories

I run and run
Down empty hallways
Haunted by lost memories

I try to grasp them
But they slip through my fingers
As if they were smoke

Childhood memories dissolving
In front of my eyes
While sadness overwhelms me

The taunting sounds
Of a time lost
Grates on my frazzled nerves

I scream in frustration
As I lose piece after piece
Of my past

Dust

It all turns to dust
In a matter of moments
Feelings lost
And unloved
Reaching for hope
Grasping only thin air
How far to come
Only to fail
Just another speck
Of silky dust

Fatigue

Sleep is an elusive mistress
Every night
We play this game
Knowing that I will rarely win
I pray that Morpheus will aid me
But he seems reluctant to fight my mistress

Night and day
I carry the burden that is fatigue
It gnaws at my limbs
At my frail mental state
It drags me down to sit or lie
More often than I wish to admit
It follows me like a shadow
Through joy and hurt

Light

She is teasing us
Showing us glimpses of light
But denying us her glory

She hides behind clouds of snow
That chase across the sky
Hiding her from our sight

Her pain makes the clouds
Weep perfect snow crystals
That slowly descend

Every time she peaks through
She hopes her daughter is treated better
Yet every time she is disappointed

So, she hides behind the clouds
Denying her daughter's children
The pleasure of her company

Pressure

There is nowhere to run, nowhere to hide
The noise is rising to an excruciating crescendo
The pressure is building, preparing to blow
Forever changing the way of the world

Fog

Where have you gone, Sweet Sanity?
I keep searching for you
But the fog is too thick
For me to see through

Where have you gone, Sweet Sanity?
I'm losing my mind
My memory is failing
Crumbling under my foundation

Where have you gone, Sweet Sanity?
Confusion is shattering my confidence
Leaving me naked and vulnerable
For all to see and judge

Where have you gone, Sweet Sanity?
Please return to me
Before my mind is lost
Forgotten by everyone

Poison

I cannot fathom
Why you would breathe
Those words

They fall from your lips
As wilted flower petals
Dripping with malice

They spread like infection
Crawling over my skin
Blackening my heart

Fireworks

Imagine the fireworks
The red and golden sparks
Showering the sky in glittering light
Reflecting in the mirror of my soul

Colours of joy and wonder
Unpredictable and exciting
Spurring me on in my life's journey

Hardship and pain we all suffer
But the ability to catch the sparks
To take life by its hand and dance
To smile through the tears
And laugh through the hurt
Is a precious gift
Few people truly accept

Let go of the expectations
Of other people's opinions of you
Let go of the control
And spin till you're dizzy
Then start your life over
A clean slate
Full of innocent confidence

Bleeding Hearts

Bleeding hearts
Tears of the sky
Darkness approaching
An unstoppable force

The beast is growling
Clawing at its cage
On the verge of escaping

Frightening powers
About to be unleashed
To wreak havoc on the world

Be ready to battle
To fight for love
And all that is good in life

Sadness

Sadness overwhelms me
Tears slowly falling upon my hands
Chasing stray thoughts in the night

Lost dreams captivating me
Teasing my senses
Fleeing before I can catch them

Cracks form in my frail heart
Threatening to spill all my secrets
To an unprepared world

Plea

Come to me, I summon thee
To hear my eternal plea
On battlefields, blood I have shed
I fall on my knees in silent tears
The battle is won
But much is lost
Cleanse my tears
Take away my pain
Valhalla awaits
In your beautiful embrace

Child's Soul

Glacier eyes searching my soul
Digging into my humanity
Finding a world without cynicism
Where compassion rules
Love flows freely and all is innocent
A child's soul
Free of adult pollution
Ready to explore the world
With new eyes and no restrictions

Excruciating Pain

Excruciating pain
Radiating from my core
I cannot dull it, nor can I hide

It haunts me night and day
My own personal stalker
Lying in wait, ready to pounce
Every time I relax

I keep it hidden
Because that is my only control
Everything else is ruled
By the pain and fog

I am not ashamed of my pain
But how can I share it?
How can you understand?
When it is there
Every second of every day

So, when you see me
You see a brilliant actress
Fighting to keep smiling
And sharing compassion

Now you say
Share your pain
We can take it
We will support you

But when enough days have gone by
You either tire of hearing the same thing
Or you simply forget
Because it is there every day

No, we would never do that

Life has taught me this brutal lesson
Many times over
As I am left behind
Yet again
So easily forgotten

So, I hide it behind my smile
Behind my support and compassion
For the rest of the world
A member of the not-so-secret society
Of invisible chronic illness

Silence

Sweet blissful silence
Calming and reassuring
Flowing like water over my senses
Lulling me into enchanted sleep
Where fairytales unfold
Like night-blooming jasmine
Under the bright moon

The One

Show me your fears
And I will show you mine
Maybe you are the one
Who will love me
And care for me
Without restrictions

You will have to go through hell
To break my walls
To convince me of your love

I am a maze
Full of fire and pain
And I do not know
How to guide you through

My fight-or-flight instinct
Is on high alert
And I'll run like a skittish mare
If I get the chance

Think of me
As a wounded animal
I'll fight you
With teeth and claws

If I cannot run
Are you my valiant knight?
The one that can sooth
My inner beast
And fight my demons?
Are you the one
Who can fathom my pain
And not break down?

New Circle

The scent of spring is in the air
The sun is shining and birds chirping
Light is banishing the darkness
As bountiful times approach

Maidens prepare to dance
In the sacred halls of nature
Bidding the spring welcome
Celebrating the return of elves and fairies

A new circle has begun

Ripping

Ripping, tearing, clawing
The silver sphere yields
To the onslaught of demonic powers
Intent on yet another innocent
Blood-red tears
Threatening to unveil
A paradise lost
In a cruel world of bloody war

Dream Land

Moonlight filters in through the blinds
In the still of the night
As I lie in my soft bed
Watching my dream catcher
Lazily turn in a calming circle

Peace settles over me
As sleep sneaks upon me
Dreams cautiously approach
Seeing if my mind is ready

To enter the lands outside of this realm
I let myself fall into the world
Of fairies and unicorns
Valkyries and Vikings
Brushing up against
The land of the Gods

How I wish I could remember
My nightly adventures
To know if they are what shapes me
Into the person I am when I'm awake
Or if they are simply an escape
From a world devoid of magic

Lost Hope

You tear out my heart
With reckless abandonment
You huff and puff
And punish without mercy
You destroy hope of love
Of future bliss
Your anger hurts me
Stripping me of my honour
Leaving me a hopeless fool
On the brink of self-destruction
In the midst of emotional turmoil

The Sting

True blue
Under the sky
Over the rainbow
Foggy mornings

Take the sting out of life
Chocolate truffles
Unicorn visions
Gnomes under ground
Elves up high

Take the sting out of life
A hug from a loved one
A kind word from a stranger
A child's laughter
A comforting tweet

Take the sting out of life

Release Me

They prey on me in the dark night
Where silence is absolute
And my mind far from calm

The voices haunt me
They taunt me
They tear me apart

There is no rest to be found
Only the chilling presence
Of ancient insanity

Icy fingers touching my spirit
Leaving me cold to the bone
By their relentless invasion

Come to me
They beckon and plea
Madness waiting to embrace me

I dare not obey
For only the abyss is there
All-consuming in the dark

I wish they would release
The tattered remains
Of my broken self

I would soar high as the mighty eagle
Above the violent storm
Raging through my mind

I would ride the wind
Soaking up the freedom
Released from the mortal chains

Crushed

Feelings crushed
Under the boot heel of oppression

Ropes tied around my spine
Tightening every second

A lesson of burning hurt
Of desperate confinement

A lost flight of life
In universal macro moments

Whiplash of bile
Ripping the skin
Leaving welts of despair
In its hellish wake

Mist

Mist rolling over the lake
Shrouding everything in mystery

The old crone is brewing
She is one of the ancient ones
Cunning and charming
Deadly to those who cross her
Belladonna and Dantura
At her beck and call

Hush Hush

Intent on sneaking out
Like a thief in the night
With my hidden treasure
Lost, as I am almost caught

Shhh

Do not say a word
Do not cry over
What you never had

Maybe in another life
In another place
Where things are different
And love is meant to be

Karma

She steps out of the night
With a dark glint in her eyes

She is the hoar frost
The harbinger of death

She comes with a message
Of karmic retribution

To those who failed
Love and compassion

Beware of her
For she is tireless

She never misses
She will find you

Blade

The sharp blade
Sliding over the skin
Cutting with precision
Deep into the heart
Twisting and tearing
Ripping my soul open

I scream and fight
But to no avail

The walls are breaking
The fortress crumbling
A lifetime of building
Gone in seconds

Can love rebuild
My broken soul?

Empty

Empty rooms
Painted with loneliness

Shattered dreams
Floating in the air

The broken hearts
Of reckless lovers
Strewn over the floor
For all to walk over
In disrespect

Thousands of bitter tears
Running down the abandoned walls
To create puddles of self-pity

Ink

The familiar pain

Vibrations

As the needle tears the skin

The ink connecting with my body

In story-telling patterns

Pap

Generous and genius
A question is a lecture waiting
A lecturer is a drawing in disguise

Ask the question
And he shall paint you a picture
Worth a million words

Teaching me
That nothing is impossible
That reaching for the stars in the sky
Isn't necessary

Because they already reside
Here on earth
Shining a blinding light
Sharing their grace
Without hesitation

Unicorn

I am the God of hellfire
And I bring you
Tiny sparkling stars in the sky
Drizzling fairy dust
Over green meadows
Filled with rainbow-colored unicorns
Feasting on chocolate rivers
Farthing lollipops and candy floss

I woke up one morning and found this unicorn poem on my phone. I must have been sleep-writing. I really wish I could remember the dream this came from.

Savage Rose

Idun

The warm spring wind in the night
Carries the scent of gentler times
Of the yellow colza fields
And sweet strawberries

The old elder trees blossoms
Herbs are breaking free of the ground
Bright green beech unfolding
And the swallow is chasing bugs

Her name is Idun
She is spring and immortality
Guardian
Of the apples of life

Mourning

My heart is bleeding
I cannot breathe
Tears burn in my eyes
And my throat hurts
Dark clouds
Hover above
Ready to cry
The tears I hold back
Too soon
The life-thread was cut
Stealing from us
A beautiful soul

Tango Jalousie

Slow... slow...
Quick, quick, slow...
You spin me around
As we push and play
The music is hypnotic
Dictating our moves
A battle of wills
On the polished floors
We turn and sway
As we express our infatuation
Passion in movement
A sparkle in the eye
Let the seduction commence

A Piece of My Soul

Darkness devours
The shadows of my mind

Silence is absolute
In the eye of the storm

I stand outside looking in
Knowing that
All hell is about to break loose

The voices start
As silent whispers
Rising in crescendo
As more and more join in

They are all desperate
Now shouting to be heard

My fingers are drumming
A tribal rhythm on the keyboard

Words flashing across the screen
Faster and faster

Thoughts and conversations
Feelings and actions
Meld into a captivating tale
Ready to be uploaded
To be shared
With fellow lovers of words

Flames

Flames licking over my skin
Pouring down my throat
Black billowing clouds
Exiting my lungs

My mind seizing
Under the burning screams
Shaking
Convulsing

The taste of blood strengthening
Caged in my own
Tormented body
Begging for mercy
For release

No
No release
Only torment

Bloody tears
I taste the bloody tears
This must be hell

Yes
My own personal hell

No escape
No redemption
Only eternal torment

How long have I been here?
Minutes
Hours
Days

I no longer remember
There is only the pain

A Lost Soul

A soul lost, love lost
But not abandoned

Picking up the pieces
To rebuild a new life
Alone

In a sea of people
No one truly understands
The pain of her heart
How completely
It has been ripped apart

The broken pieces
Filled with impossible longing
Leaving her breathless
Twilight, dawn, and dusk

How does she mend
This gaping hole in her soul?

The ragged edges
Painful and bleeding
Where her soul's completion
Was ripped away

Leaving her alone
In a cold world
Without his warmth
Without his touch

An open wound
Waiting to close
Hopefully healing
But never forgetting

Take Me Away

Take me away
To the land of dragons and castles
I don't want to be a grown-up anymore
I want to frolic in a Fairyland
And forget all about the real world
Of pain and hard decisions
I want to be a child again
To see the adventures around every corner
To believe in the impossible
A return to innocence
To a carefree life
Where all is possible

Eurus

A storm is coming
I wait patiently for it
For the rain to fall
And cleanse me
With my feet planted
Firmly in the mud
Connecting with
Mother Earth
The eastern wind
Gently drying me
Breathing new life
Into me
As the clouds part
To let the sun
Warm me
Inside and out

My Demon

He sits on my back, night'n day
Gnawing and clawing
Whispering taunts in my ear
Poisoning my body and soul
Whenever my guard is down
He steals bits and pieces of me
At night he keeps me awake with his wailing
At day he hums a lullaby
When I speak, he steals my words
When I'm silent, he speaks for me
When I walk, he trips me
When I sit, he makes me twitch
He's a dark shadow
Neither evil nor good
He's my constant companion
My own personal demon

Asterix

A brave little warrior
With a deceptively
Sweet appearance
A champion of the gods
In a tiny body
With a hint of madness
Full of love
And endless cuddles
Night and day
Favoured by Neptune
A little sailor
Drifting into the sunset

Frozen Pictures

Pictures frozen in time
That's how I remember you
A young man with big plans
And youthful dreams

You swept me off my feet
Teaching me to dream big
Showing me the world
And a foreign life

But I was a young girl
Being overwhelmed
Everything moving too fast
For this simple country girl

Breaking your heart
Was a dark day in my life
Though I do not regret
Following my instincts
We were too young
And too naïve

Mad Love

Your love tastes of madness
Insanity rolling on my tongue
Breathing down my throat
Obsession colours your touch
Demanding my attention
As you take what you want
I am helpless in my pleasure
Writhing under your expert touch
And watchful eye
You deliver sweet pain
Craving submission
That I am reluctant to give

Enough

Choose your weapon
And make your choice wisely
For I have no mercy left in me
Only bloodlust and iron will

I will have my revenge
Let the battle commence
So, I can celebrate my victory

You have stepped on me
For the last time
I am no longer your victim
I am your judge, jury, and executioner

Rejoice in the fact
That it will be a swift death
I have no use for your begging
Only your final ending

I'll purge you from my memories
From my broken heart
And torn emotions

It will be as if you never existed
Never brought your hate and ignorance
Into my gentle life

Reflection

I no longer recognize
The reflection in the mirror

Where has the sparkling
Young lady gone?
Who is that woman?

The one that always looks tired
With the blue circles around the eyes
And the pale, almost translucent skin
Slightly hunched shoulders
Looking defeated

She rarely smiles at me
She just looks lost

Where did she come from?
I certainly didn't invite her in

Sometimes, I see glimpses
Of the happy, carefree young woman

But she disappears
Almost as soon as she appears

I wonder where she goes,
If she will ever return

Maybe she lives in the mirror
Waiting for me to appear
Waiting for her chance
To tease and taunt me

Misery

Crushed
Onto an unforgiving wall
Of pity and sorrow

All strength gone
Shrouded in misery

An unforgiving cloak
Squeezing pain
Out of my eyes

Amour

One ~ two

Amour ~ amour

Sultry summer nights

With a scent of jasmine

Hot air caressing

My bare skin

Your breath on my neck

Your hand in my hair

Waves lapping

Gently at our feet

As we sway in tune

With Ægir's song

Dreamer

I’m a dreamer
I sit on my couch
Looking out the window
Watching the clouds move and sway
Igniting my imagination

There is no time limit
As to how long I can sit there
Letting my mind play
Tuning out everyday life

As I frolic in Summerland
My imagination is on the loose
Amongst dragons and fawns
Kitty cats and chocolate dreams

In colourful lands beyond this reality
Everything is possible
I'm not inhibited
By my body's limitations

I invite you to join me
To dance in the clouds
To battle evil and rescue the innocent
To make fairytales come true

Sunrise ~ Sunset

It all starts with a sunrise
Bright yellow and candy floss pink
Bidding good morning
To the birth of a new day
Of a new chance
To fulfil your dreams
To reinvent yourself
And make amends

When the day ends
And the night approaches
The sunset dazzles us
With red and golden hues
Leaving us in awe
Of the wonder that is nature

Another day passes
New life lessons learned
With victories and mistakes
Under our belt

We say good night

And kiss our loved ones

Hoping for blissful sleep

Preparing us for yet another day

For it all to start over

Bathed in golden sunlight

Captive

Touch me
Kiss me
Hold me
Breathe me in
Before you slay me
With your acidic words
I crave your touch
As well as your abuse
You own me
Body and soul
As soon as my feet
Leave the ground
You whip me down
I cannot free myself from you
The ropes tighten
Minute by minute

Nightmare

I am the thoughts
That creep under the skin
In the darkest of hours
When we feel most alone
And the silence is absolute

I'll twist and turn your thoughts
Until you don't know up or down
And the nightmare is riding your soul
Into the pitch-black abyss
Where the terrifying unknown awaits

The Bell Chimes

The bell chimes
For the lost Homo sapiens
That walk this tormented earth
The seasons are rapidly changing
As we, in our hunt for riches,
Desecrate the world
Famine and war
Ignorance and cruelty
Is everyday life
What have we become
To be this heartless?
Ignoring our fellow travellers suffering
Turning a blind eye
To everything
But our selfish wants
How easily we have forgotten
Our compassion
And precious humanity

Northern Wind

My heart beats slow and steady
In perfect tune with nature
As my soul plays catch
With the Borea Ohio

I feel the steady hum
Of the earth in my bones

Twirling like a leaf in the wind
I listen to the ancient voices of the trees
Of silver streams
And the animal life in the woods

I hear them all
Mixing into a natural hymn
A hymn that beats
To the rhythm of my heart

Hailstorm

Hailstorm
In an hourglass
Counting down
Hail by hail
In a steady tempo
Far and beyond
It's all the same
One by one
They drop through
Life's hourglass
Counting the years
In light-speed
Only one breath away
From eternal sleep
Fast forgotten

Burn for You

I burn for you
Your touch, my command
And soul my twin

I rage for you
Your guardian angel
And saviour

I weep for you
Your insufferable pain
And hardship

I scream for you
Your fight against injustice
And prejudice

I cheer for you
Your incredible courage
And smiles

Song of the Whales

The warm water makes small sounds
As it licks the sand between my toes
The moonlight shines bright at the surface
Making it look like hammered silver
An intense yearning
Has overtaken my heart
The longing to be one with the sea
To move through it effortlessly
To watch the moon beams
Penetrate the silky surface
While navigating the dark depth
Side by side with gentle giants
Joining them
As they break the surface
To breathe and play
Creating waves with their big tails
Sharing the knowledge
Of an endless universe

Cold

Wind sweeping
Across my face
Flashing colours
The blackbird sings
The sun is gone
Only the cold is left
Shivering
Hugging myself
Wondering
When will it end?

Lesson

I have learnt my lesson
Burnt my fingers
Torched my soul
Fractured my heart
On your broken promises
Things are not meant to be this hard
Why do you have to complicate it all?
Just accept what you cannot feel
Instead of thinking that you know better
Than my real life experiences
Your theories are badly flawed
But your pride and confidence
Prevents you from seeing it
So, you lecture and despise me
When things don't work as you see fit
I do not deserve this
And will not accept it
This stops now
Before we break each other
And make it impossible to ever heal

Devil's Dance

I dance through a thousand deaths
Little neurons extinguished
As I play amongst the stars
To the song of the nightingales

Come dance with me
Through the devil's footsteps
On the black shores
Below the raging storm

I'll seduce you
With the music of my soul
And carnal pleasures
Towards the final death

I am the night
My name is whispered with fear
In the dark shadows
Woman

Bystander

No emotions whatsoever
Only an empty void
Filled with bitter darkness

Time flows as a roaring river
With me standing on the bank
Watching in silent despair

If only I could jump in the river
Following life as I ought to
As everyone streams by me

Instead, I stand silent
Unable to move
On the cursed riverbank

Garden Joys

I stroll through the garden
Surrounded by colours and scents
That are a soothing balm for my soul

The grass is soft and cool
Beneath my bare feet
The sun caressing my skin

Butterflies and bees
Add to the charms
Of this paradise on earth

I feel at peace
The voices quiet
My being relaxed

No Redemption

Come fly with me
Come die with me
Over the hills
Into the valleys
Spreading my wings
Unsheathing my sword
Causing terror
In black hearts
No redemption
Only the verdict

Sunshine

Sunshine, lollipops, and lemon drops
Happy thoughts and puppy love
How can that not make you smile?

Sunset cuddles and moonlit kisses
Dancing in the summer rain
How can that not make you feel?

Falling stars and sand between my toes
The smell of the ocean on a stormy day

How can that not make you see
That love and happiness conquer it all
For you and me

Fragile

I'm fragile, brittle to the bone
Delicate like a China doll
Despite my appearance
But my mind is strong
How else would I survive?
Give me some credit
For handling people's discriminations
Without twitching
Without becoming bitter
And lashing out

Naughty

I do very bad things
And I do them very well
They make my little black heart
Skip with delight
Licking and kicking
Writhing on rumpled sheets
Tie me up
Tie me down
Let me crawl under your skin
And darken your heart
Showing you unspeakable pleasures
Of which you never dreamt

Shadows

As I walk through the night
The ink-black shadows
Conceal my state of mind
Lulling me into a false security
I forget the painful truths
That the harsh daylight
Shines upon me
Weakness and wants
Pain and regrets
Slap me in the face
As life yet again
Kicks me in my teeth
I pull the darkness around me
Like an impenetrable cocoon
Soft denial comforting me
Devouring my insecurities
The night is calm
It belongs to me
A soothing balm
To a troubled day

Silence

Silence after the storm
Golden lights
Bathe the world
In their healing rays
Bringing hope
Of better times
Of love and compassion
And a bright future

Fire Soul

Intense and intelligent
No battle too big or too small
Always on the move
But always time to share
A kind word to everyone
A gentle heart
All encompassing
Making an impression
Impossible to forget
Yes, I will never forget
This fire soul
That roamed this earth
For a way too short time
Leaving behind
An impressive footprint
Teaching us all
To live and love
Right now, and not tomorrow

Acknowledgements

In loving memory of Morten 1969- 2013

Thank you Melissa Craig, for inspiring me to write. Thank you Ben Ditmars, for all your help and advice. You gave me the courage to share this book with the world. You rock! Thank you to my wonderful beta readers Kim Stapf and Kat McCarthy.

About Helle Gade

Helle Gade lives in Denmark with her little diva dog. She is a book blogger, poet, photographer, nocturnal creature, avid reader and chocolate addict. She has been writing poetry since 2011 and published four poetry collections since then. She has been fortunate to work with a bunch of brilliant authors and photographers on The Mind's Eye series. Her book Nocturnal Embers won the Best Poetry Collection with eFestival of Words.

Other BDP books by Helle Gade

Terrifying Love - A Halloween Anthology

Beautiful Tragedy - A Halloween Anthology

Poesi - A Collection of Poems Volume One

Dolce Amore

The Fighter